Henry Hudson

Discover The Life Of An Explorer

Trish Kline

Rourke

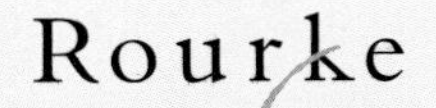

Publishing LLC

Vero Beach, Florida 32964

www.rourkepublishing.com

PHOTO CREDITS: IRC-www.historypictures.com: cover, pages 10, 13, 14, 17, 18; © Hulton/Archive by Getty Images: title page, pages 4, 15; © The Canadian Heritage Gallery: pages 8, 21; © Artville: page 7.

Title page: American Indians met Hudson's arrival with caution.

Editor: Frank Sloan

Cover design by Nicola Stratford

Library of Congress Cataloging-in-Publication Data

Kline, Trish
Henry Hudson / Trish Kline.
p. cm. — (Discover the life of an explorer)
Summary: Introduces the life of Henry Hudson, the English sea captain who explored the Arctic Ocean and the river and bay later named for him while in search of a northern route to the Orient.
Includes bibliographical references and index.
ISBN 1-58952-296-6
1. Hudson, Henry, d. 1611—Juvenile literature. 2. America—Discovery and exploration—English—Juvenile literature. 3. Explorers—America—Biography—Juvenile literature. 4. Explorers—Great Britain—Biography—Juvenile literature. [1. Hudson, Henry, d. 1611. 2. Explorers. 3. America—Discovery and exploration—English.] I. Title.

E129.H8 K58 2002
910'.92—dc21
[B] 2002020708

Printed in the USA

CG/CG

TABLE OF CONTENTS

Man of the Sea	5
First Voyage	6
The Arctic's Cold Waters	9
A New Goal	11
Frozen!	16
Mutiny	19
Famous Discoveries	20
Important Dates to Remember	22
Glossary	23
Index	24
Further Reading/Websites to Visit	24

MAN OF THE SEA

Henry Hudson was born about 1570 near London, England. Not much is known about his youth. But when he was very young, his life was on the seas. In 1588, he was aboard an English ship fighting the Spanish. Later, he sailed to the North Sea and Africa. On these trips, he traded steel axes for gold and spices.

Henry Hudson's early years prepared him for exploration.

FIRST VOYAGE

In 1607, Hudson sailed on his first **voyage** of discovery. He sailed the ship *Hopewell* from England to the shores of present-day Greenland. Hudson was searching for a water pathway to East Asia. He did not find this **Northeast Passage**. A year later, he tried once more. But, again, he failed.

Henry Hudson was hired to find a Northeast Passage to Asia.

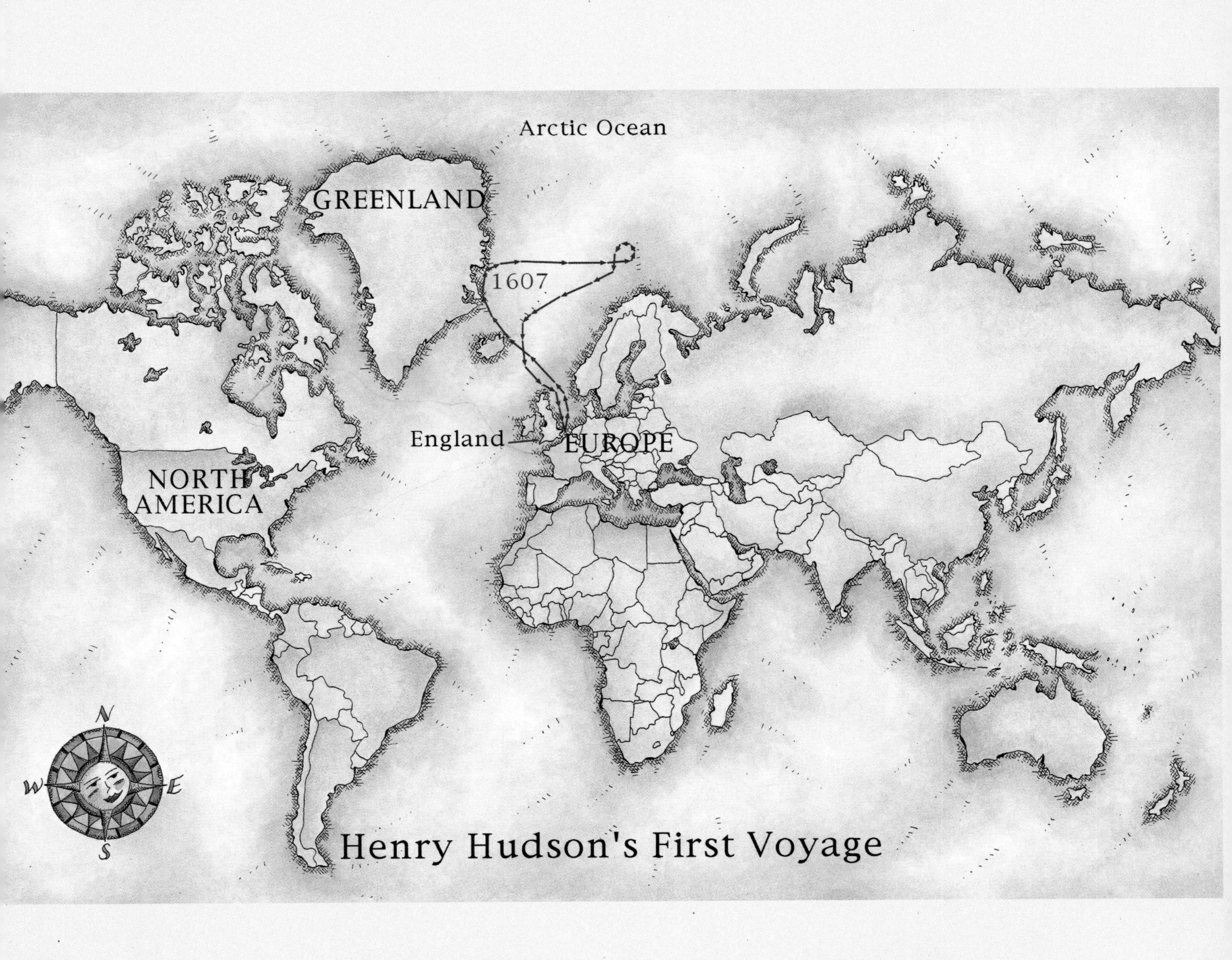

Arctic Ocean
GREENLAND
1607
England
EUROPE
NORTH AMERICA
N
W
E
S
Henry Hudson's First Voyage

THE ARCTIC'S COLD WATERS

In 1609, Hudson sailed on his third voyage. On the ship *Half Moon*, Hudson sailed north. Soon, he was in waters of the Arctic Ocean. The weather was cold. Hudson had to **navigate** the ship around large pieces of ice. The crew was unhappy. They talked about taking over the ship.

Large icebergs made Hudson's voyage dangerous.

A NEW GOAL

Hudson decided to change his goal. He would give up his search for a Northeast Passage. Instead, he would find a **Northwest Passage** to China. This change of plans brought Hudson to the shores of the New World.

Natives watch Hudson's ship enter Delaware Bay.

Hudson sailed the *Half Moon* across the Atlantic Ocean. He sailed north into present-day Delaware Bay. There, Hudson found a wide river. He thought that this river was a **passage** to the Pacific Ocean.

Hudson sailed his ship up the river. But, this river was not the passage to the Pacific Ocean.

Hudson went ashore to meet the natives.

Hudson's crew experienced many hardships during their long voyage.

Hudson offered gifts to natives along the river.

FROZEN!

In 1610, Hudson set sail on his fourth voyage. His new ship was named the *Discovery*. Again, he hoped to find a Northwest Passage. By mid-year, he had reached what we now know as Hudson Bay. There, he spent three months exploring the islands.

Winter soon arrived. The *Discovery* was frozen in for the winter. Hudson could not sail south to warmer waters. The winter was very cold. The crew grew unhappy. Hudson faced a crew ready to **mutiny.**

Hudson and his crew explored the islands around Hudson Bay.

MUTINY

This time, Hudson could not stop the mutiny. In the early spring of 1611, the crew took over the ship. They put Hudson in a small boat and pushed it away from the ship. The *Discovery* sailed away.

When the ship reached England, the crew was arrested. They were put in prison. Henry Hudson was never seen again.

Hudson and a few loyal members of his crew were set adrift in the spring of 1611.

FAMOUS DISCOVERIES

Henry Hudson is famous for having made four voyages of discovery. Though he never found a Northwest Passage, both a river and bay are named for him. These are the Hudson River and Hudson Bay.

Hudson and his small group of supporters were never seen again.

IMPORTANT DATES TO REMEMBER

1570?	Born in England
1588	Fought the Spanish at sea
1607	Sailed on first voyage of discovery
1609	Sailed the waters of the Arctic Ocean
1610	Discovered Hudson Bay
1611	Disappeared at sea

GLOSSARY

mutiny (MYOOT nee) — to turn against the person in charge, such as a crew turning against a ship's captain

navigate (NAV i gayt) — to steer the way you want to go

Northeast Passage (NORTH eest PAS ij) — a water pathway to East Asia

Northwest Passage (NORTH west PAS ij) — a pathway to China

passage (PAS ij) — a path through which something may pass

voyage (VOY ij) — a trip to a faraway place

INDEX

Arctic Ocean 9
Atlantic Ocean 12
born 5
mutiny 16, 19
Northeast Passage 6, 11
Northwest Passage 11, 16, 20
Pacific Ocean 12
voyage 6, 9, 16, 20

Further Reading

Goodman, Joan Elizabeth. *Beyond the Sea of Ice: Voyages of Henry Hudson*. Mikaya Press, 1999.
Mattern, Joanne. *The Travels of Henry Hudson*. Raintree Steck-Vaughn, 2000.
Santella, Andrew. *Henry Hudson*. Franklin Watts, 2001.

Websites To Visit

http://www.pbs.org
http://www.mariner.org (The Mariner's Museum, Newport News, VA)
http://www.ianchadwick.com/hudson

About The Author

Trish Kline has written a great number of nonfiction books for the school and library market. Her publishing credits include two dozen books, as well as hundreds of newspaper and magazine articles, anthologies, short stories, poetry, and plays. She lives in Helena, Montana.